ARIZONA
CHILD
CUSTODY
ESSENTIALS
What Every Parent
Needs To Know

ARIZONA
CHILD
CUSTODY
ESSENTIALS
**What Every Parent
Needs To Know**

Scott David Stewart, Esq.
Amy E. Dohrendorf, Esq.

An Imprint of Stewart Law Group
www.ArizonaLawGroup.com

Published in 2015 by Stewart Law Group USA

• 777 E Thomas Rd Ste 210, Phoenix AZ 85014 •
• 1490 S Price Rd Ste 212, Chandler AZ 85286 •
• 17470 N Pacesetter Way, Scottsdale AZ 85255 •
• 14050 N 83rd Ave Ste 290, Peoria AZ 85381 •
• 1910 S Stapley Dr Ste 221, Mesa AZ 85204 •
• 20325 N 51st Ave Ste 134, Glendale AZ 85308 •

www.arizonalawgroup.com

FIRST EDITION

ISBN   978-0-9886052-3-7

For information please write:
Stewart Law Group
777 E Thomas Rd Ste 210
Phoenix AZ 85014

Legal Disclaimer

The general information in this book is not, nor is it intended to be, specific legal advice. You should consult an attorney for specific legal advice regarding your individual situation.

This book is provided as a general reference work and is for informational purposes only. You are advised to check for changes to current law and to consult with a qualified attorney on any legal issue. The receipt of or use of this book does not create an attorney-client relationship with Stewart Law Group or any of its attorneys.

Because this book was prepared for a general readership, without investigation into the facts of each particular case, it is not legal advice. Neither Stewart Law Group nor any of its attorneys has an attorney-client relationship with you. The thoughts and commentary about the law contained in this book are provided merely as a public service and do not constitute solicitation or legal advice.

While we endeavored to provide accurate information in this book, we cannot guarantee that the material provided herein is accurate, adequate, or complete. This general legal information is provided on an 'as-is' basis. We make no warranties and disclaim liability for damages resulting from its use. Legal advice must be tailored to the specific circumstances of each case and laws are constantly changing, therefore nothing provided in this book should be used as a substitute for the advice of competent counsel. The material in this book may be considered advertising under applicable rules.

The law in Arizona has changed in that the term "child custody" is no longer used. In its place, Arizona law now uses legal decision-making and parenting time. However, because child custody is still in common use and is recognized by most people, we continue to use it in this book when referring to global issues in a general sense. In all other discussions, we use the terms "legal decision-making" and "parenting time" specifically.

Contents

I

Introduction to Child Custody Proceedings in Arizona

This short book is essential reading for every parent who anticipates, or already has pending, a child custody case in Arizona's family court system. Because the outcome of every custody decision could have an impact on your children's welfare and future happiness, there are many legal concepts and proceedings to learn about.

To start with, both parents have rights and responsibilities regarding the care, maintenance, and support of their minor children. But there are common misconceptions about what the law requires of parents.

For example, did you know that child support does not always end when the child reaches the age of majority? Support is typically ordered through the child's high school graduation, even after age 18. And for a disabled child who will turn 18 before the divorce is final, support may be ordered well beyond that child's majority. Don't let your parenting decisions be guided by erroneous information!

Although not a substitute for competent legal advice from an Arizona licensed attorney, *Arizona Child Custody Essentials* can help prepare and guide you through the proceedings ahead. In this book, you will learn about:

- The child custody process under Arizona law;

- The judge's responsibilities, powers, and discretion;

- The roles of child custody evaluators, mediators, and parenting coordinators;

- The value of a good parenting plan; and

- Many useful tips to help you through the proceedings and with parenting time thereafter.

As a parent, deciding what is in the best interests of your children will be among the most important decisions you will ever make. Some of those decisions will come easily, but many others will be challenging for both parties. Of course, there is a strong emotional component to every child custody case, whether decisions are made for one child or several children. And when custody is contested, the stresses, delays, and costs associated with court proceedings can seem to increase exponentially.

The best preparation for your case is to learn everything you can about Arizona's child custody laws and proceedings. With that goal in mind, this book will demystify the custody process and help you build a solid foundation for legal decision-making.

Before getting started, note that in Arizona law the term "child custody" is no longer used. In its place are legal decision-making and parenting time. Having said that, because child custody is still in common use and is recognized by most people, we continue to use it in this book when referring to global issues in a general sense. In all other discussions, we use the term "legal decision-making" and "parenting time" specifically.

Also, we included selected Arizona statutes at the end of the book for easy reference. Be mindful, though, that laws can change. Always talk to your attorney about what the law is as applied to your case.

Arizona Child Custody Essentials

2

Arizona Jurisdiction Over Child Custody

How do you know if child custody will be an issue in your case? Custody proceedings are a part of every family law matter involving children. Parenting issues can arise out of a couple's divorce, legal separation, annulment, or follow an establishment of paternity.

Therefore, if you have minor children, custody decisions must be made. Once the court asserts jurisdiction, the Superior Court Judge will render a final custody decision and issue orders accordingly. Those orders will cover child support, parenting time, and legal decision-making authority. A.R.S. § 25-402.

Why Is Jurisdiction Important?

Before an Arizona court will hear the family law case, make decisions, and issue orders, it must have proper jurisdiction, or authority. The court must have:

- Jurisdiction over the subject matter of the lawsuit;

- Jurisdiction over both parties to the lawsuit;

- Jurisdiction over custody under the Uniform Child Custody Jurisdiction and Enforcement Act (UCCJEA); and

- Jurisdiction over property and things located in Arizona.

What happens when Arizona lacks jurisdiction? Well, then the case must be filed in the state that has jurisdiction. Let's take a closer look at each of these so you understand why establishing jurisdiction is an essential first step.

Subject Matter Jurisdiction:

Under our state constitution, domestic relations cases – divorce, legal separation, child custody, child support, and annulment – are the original subject matter of Arizona's Superior Courts. The Superior Court cannot hear a case when subject matter jurisdiction is not present, even if both parties want the court to hear the case. Arizona Constitution, Article VI § 14.

Jurisdiction Over Parties:

Think of this as Arizona's reasonable connection to the people asking it for a final judgment. For example, if a spouse files for divorce here, then one of the spouses must have been domiciled in Arizona (or stationed here if a service member) as a permanent resident for 90 days or longer before the court has jurisdiction. Often it is only a matter of waiting a little longer before filing for divorce, so that personal jurisdiction can be established. A.R.S. § 25-312.

UCCJEA:

Specific to custody, we have the **Arizona Uniform Child Custody Jurisdiction and Enforcement Act**. A.R.S. § 25-1031. This is just a brief overview, but the Superior Court's authority to make an initial child custody determination or decision on parenting time is dependent upon whether:

1. Arizona is where the child has lived for the most recent six months ("home state" jurisdiction); or

2. Arizona has the most significant connection with the child and at least one parent, in terms

of evidence, contacts, and the like; or

3. The child is physically present in Arizona and needs protection because of abandonment or some emergency; or

4. No other state is able to assert jurisdiction, or chooses to assert jurisdiction if it could, and it is in the child's best interests for Arizona to assume jurisdiction.

If none of those circumstances exist, then the court lacks jurisdiction over the child and will dismiss the custody case.

Jurisdiction Over Property and Things:

This "in rem" jurisdiction is the court's power over the parties' property and assets located in Arizona. The court exercises in rem jurisdiction in every divorce when it divides the couple's property.

With jurisdiction established, the next step is to decide on the proper **venue** – that is, which Arizona county to file with. If both spouses reside in Phoenix, for example, then proper venue for their divorce would ordinarily be the Superior Court of Arizona in Maricopa County. Regardless of venue, whenever a party asks the court to determine legal decision-making and specific parenting time, both parents must complete the mandatory **parent information program**. A.R.S. § 25-351.

Stewart Law Group

3

Hiring Your Arizona Child Custody Lawyer

Selecting your Arizona child custody lawyer may be among the most important decisions you will ever make. You want the best possible results in your case, so choose your lawyer well. You also want to be confident in the representation and in the legal proceedings.

Before you hire the lawyer, ask these six questions:

1. *Do you have substantial experience with contested child custody matters?*

2. *What attorney credentials do you bring to the*

representation?

3. *Have you ever been sanctioned for an attorney ethics violation?*

4. *Will you handle my custody case or will it be turned over to another attorney at the firm?*

5. *How much will the legal representation cost?*

6. *Will I receive copies of every document in my case and will my calls be returned promptly?*

Be sure the attorney you hire listens carefully to your concerns and answers your questions directly. Search for a professional in whom you feel comfortable placing your trust with the most important people in your life, your children.

I. Do You Have Substantial Experience with Contested Child Custody Matters?

In Arizona, legal decision-making is awarded to the parent whom the court believes will act in accordance with the child's best interests. There is no legal presumption favoring one parent over the other. Therefore, if you desire legal decision-making authority or substantial parenting time, it is essential that your lawyer be experienced with contested child custody matters.

At Stewart Law Group, we believe child custody is best settled through voluntary agreement between parents. But custody is often hotly contested and parenting agreements are not always possible. We know from over 65 years of combined legal experience that custody cases are often protracted, requiring intensive litigation. Our lawyers are prepared to take whatever legal action is necessary to help you get the best custody arrangement possible.

Many custody procedures are used to help determine what is best for a child, namely mediation, parenting conferences, child custody evaluations, and settlement conferences. The child may have legal advocates, too. A best interests attorney and child's attorney could be appointed to represent the minor throughout the court proceedings. Our family law team has ample experience with all of these custody matters and with the practitioners associated with them.

2. What Attorney Credentials Do You Bring to the Representation?

Your child custody lawyer must be knowledgeable about Arizona's laws and the federal laws affecting your case. Be sure to examine the profiles and credentials of the entire law firm – from partners, to associates, to paralegals. With a little online research into the firm's website and by simply asking the right questions, you can determine whether the attorney and law firm have the best credentials.

The author, Scott Stewart, is an attorney in good standing with the State Bar of Arizona, and a member of the Maricopa County Bar Association, the American Bar Association, and others. He is also an AV®-rated attorney in the Martindale-Hubbell Peer Review and rated "Superb" by Avvo.com. Each of our attorneys is highly qualified and dedicated to carrying out the firm's mission and to upholding the firm's reputation for excellence in the practice of divorce and family law. Every member of our legal team is concerned with providing the best customer service possible to our clients.

3. Have You Ever Been Sanctioned for an Attorney Ethics Violation?

Attorneys are held to high ethical standards with regard to the practice of law and to the customer service they provide to their clients. The State Bar of Arizona regulates all of its lawyer members, disciplining for acts of professional misconduct. A grievance filed against an attorney could result in reprimand, probation, suspension, restitution, or disbarment revoking the lawyer's license to practice law in Arizona. You need assurance as to the moral character and legal competency of your lawyer. If the lawyer has been sanctioned for an attorney ethics violation, then you need to find out about it sooner rather than later.

Practicing law with the utmost degree of ethics is at our firm's core. At Stewart Law Group, we take great pride in our reputation for high professional ethical standards and successful, experienced, dedicated family law representation for our clients. Not one of our lawyers has ever been found to have violated an attorney ethics rule.

4. Will You Handle My Custody Case or Will It Be Turned Over to Another Attorney with the Firm?

At some law firms, the attorney you meet at the initial consultation will not be the lawyer representing you in court. If you interview one attorney, but will be represented by another at the firm, then insist on meeting with the lawyer who will actually represent you and handle the custody case. How else can you assess whether the communication necessary for a positive outcome is even possible?

At Stewart Law Group, the attorney you meet at the initial interview – and with whom you enter into a signed retainer agreement – will be the lawyer representing you throughout your custody matter. Each of our attorneys develops a core relationship of trust with their clients. This relationship requires direct, open, and frequent communication between the two of you.

5. How Much Will the Legal Representation Cost?

Never shy away from asking this important question. Ask how much you will be charged for lawyer services and what the retainer fee will be, if any. Managing legal expenses requires planning and budgeting, so you need to know in advance what the attorney's billing practices are. Some lawyer statements cover months of services, resulting in surprisingly large bills that could exceed the funds you carefully set aside for legal expenses.

Other attorneys charge a premium rate for their court appearances. Ask how the lawyer's time will be billed when working on your custody case. Some law firms charge a minimum fee for any task, regardless of whether the work took the lawyer two minutes or 15.

At our law firm, we want every client to make an informed decision and be completely comfortable with our fee structure. Therefore, a discussion about the cost of legal representation always precedes any signed representation agreement. We carefully explain our billing system and when payments are due. The client is never surprised with hidden expenses or unexpected legal fees.

We explain any costs and fees necessarily required in the custody matter. We discuss our payment options, which can help the client stay in control of legal expenses. Our invoices are sent out once a month, ensuring the client is aware of the work performed, how much time the work took to complete, and what the cost was. At our firm, we do not charge higher rates for appearing in court on behalf of a client – our attorney rates always remain the same. These are precisely the kind of up-front cost disclosures you deserve to know before you hire a lawyer.

6. Will I Receive Copies of Every Document in My Case and Will My Calls Be Returned Promptly?

Does the attorney and law firm have adequate internal management systems in place to assure that you always know what is happening in your case? Will you be able to reach your attorney when you need to, without unreasonable delay?

Remember to ask how the law firm assures your access to all case documents whenever you need them. Some attorneys systemically fail to provide clients with copies of filed court papers, motions, court orders, or correspondences between attorneys. Nothing is more worrisome than not knowing what has transpired in your custody case or being told to respond to pleadings that you have not seen and know nothing about. To make matters worse, some lawyers chronically fail to return their client's telephone calls within a reasonable time.

We make the best use of the most current technology at the Stewart Law Group to keep our clients fully engaged in their family law case. Additionally, substantive and procedural information on almost every topic in divorce and family law is readily available to clients on our website, so they can learn about any family law subject any time at no additional cost.

We send copies to the client of all case-related documents that arrived at or left our office. If a client calls when the attorney is not immediately available, then the call will be returned within 24 hours. That's the kind of outstanding customer service that our clients highly value and something you should look for in your attorney.

If the answers you get to the six questions above leave you with doubts, then continue looking elsewhere for competent legal representation and responsible customer service.

4

Unwed Parents and Paternity Establishment

For unwed mothers and fathers, child custody proceedings may follow the establishment of paternity.

Unmarried parents may voluntarily sign an Affidavit Acknowledging Paternity in Arizona, even if the child was born in another state. When paternity is uncertain or disputed, either party may seek a court order for genetic testing. If DNA test results are a match with 95% or greater certainty, then the man is presumed to be the child's biological father and the court may issue an Order of Paternity.

It's important to note that, even with a 95% DNA match, paternity could be opposed with clear and convincing evidence. A.R.S. § 25-807.

Once paternity is established, by voluntary acknowledgment or court order, child support will be ordered and custody proceedings may commence. In Arizona, both parents have an obligation to support their offspring, not just the father. Furthermore, the father has a fundamental right to custody equal with that of the mother, which includes access to his son or daughter. This means the father can seek legal decision-making authority and parenting time even though he was never married to his child's mother.

5

Key Arizona Child Custody Concepts

There are several key legal concepts associated with child custody, namely legal decision-making authority, parenting time, and visitation. (A discussion of Parenting Plans will follow in the next chapter.)

You may not be aware of this, but many of Arizona's child custody statutes were recently revised. Those changes took effect on January 1, 2013. Although we use the current statutory language in this book, do be aware that many of the older terms used prior to 2013 (such as "legal custody" and "physical custody") can still be found in other publications.

What Is Legal Decision-Making Authority?

A parent who has legal decision-making authority has the legal right and responsibility to make all non-emergency legal decisions regarding the child. (In other jurisdictions, this is sometimes referred to as legal custody.) A.R.S. § 25-401.

Those non-emergency legal decisions can have a profound impact on the child's upbringing and should be carefully considered. They include major decisions for the child's healthcare, education, personal care, and the faith the child will be brought up in (including religious training), although that is not an exclusive list.

In any Arizona child custody case, there are two possibilities: one parent is awarded sole legal decision-making or both parents are awarded joint legal decision-making.

Sole Legal Decision-Making:

When one party is granted sole legal decision-making, only that parent has legal authority to make major decisions for the child. He or she will have the legal right and responsibility to determine how important decisions over education, healthcare, personal care, and religious training will be made. Not only is making these major decisions the parent's right, he or she has a duty to make those legal decisions when the need or circumstances require.

Joint Legal Decision-Making:

The most common arrangement for Arizona families is joint legal decision-making. (Also known as joint legal custody in other jurisdictions.)

With this arrangement, the parents have equal authority to make non-emergency legal decisions over important child-rearing matters. The statute makes clear that neither party enjoys a superior position over the other when joint legal decision-making is ordered. Instead, the parents have the same rights and responsibilities. They are in an equal legal position, even if they don't always see eye-to-eye on the best course of action.

For parents who may not want equal legal authority over every major decision, there is some flexibility. There is an exception to the pure form of joint legal decision-making discussed in the previous paragraph. In the final order the judge may, for various reasons including the parents' agreement, specifically limit the scope of each parent's legal decision-making authority.

By way of example only, the parties could agree and the judge could order, that the father (an educator) shall make major decisions regarding the child's education, the mother (a children's pastor) shall make major decisions regarding the child's religious training, and both father and mother shall jointly make legal decisions regarding their child's healthcare and personal care.

Legal Decision-Making in Child's Best Interests:

The family law judge will determine which parent, or whether both parents, shall have legal decision-making authority based upon what is in the best interests of the child – physically and emotionally. A.R.S. § 25-403.

These are some of the factors the court will consider when determining legal decision-making authority:

- Relationship between parent and child (past, present, and future);

- Interrelationships and interactions between child and parents, siblings, and other persons significant to that child;

- Child's adjustment to home, school, and community;

- Child's wishes, if of suitable age and maturity;

- Mental and physical health of everyone involved;

- Parent more likely to allow substantial, meaningful, continuing, frequent contact between the child and the other parent;

- Whether a parent intentionally misled the court to gain a custody advantage;

- History of domestic violence or child abuse;

- Voluntariness of any parenting agreement;

- False reports of child abuse or neglect by a parent; and the

- Parents' ability to cooperate with joint legal decision-making.

Be mindful that the judge has considerable discretion in these matters and may consider any factor relevant to the child's physical, emotional, and moral well-being.

What Is Parenting Time?

Parenting time refers to the time the child will spend with each parent. This is the parent's scheduled access time (sometimes referred to as physical custody). Joint legal decision-making authority does not mean the parents will have equal parenting time, those are two distinct custody issues.

During parenting time, the father or mother must provide the child in his or her care with food, clothing, and shelter. A parent makes routine decisions during parenting time, but will also make emergency decisions if the child is sick or injured, for instance.

What Is Visitation?

Many people confuse visitation with parenting time, but they are not the same thing. On the one hand, only legal parents get parenting time. On the other hand, visitation is scheduled time for someone other than a parent – a grandparent, step-parent, or other important adult figure to the child. A.R.S. § 25-401(7).

For grandparents and non-parents seeking access to the child, the process of petitioning the court for visitation differs from that required of legal parents. Grandparents and third parties who are important adult figures in the child's life – adults who stand in loco parentis to the child – may ask the court for visitation. Under certain circumstances, the court could award legal decision-making authority or the placement of a child with a third party. A.R.S. § 25-409.

Can Supervised Parenting Time or Supervised Visitation Be Ordered?

In some cases, the court will order supervised parenting time or supervised visitation. The adult's time with the child may need oversight by a third party, mainly because the child's health or emotional development could be endangered if continuing supervision is not provided.

Consider the family with a history of domestic violence or potential for child abuse or neglect. Or where one parent threatened to abduct and remove the child from the jurisdiction. In those circumstances, for example, the court may decide it is in the child's best interests to order supervised adult access.

Generally, supervision is provided by a local social services agency. The expense of such supervision may be borne by one or both parties, depending upon what the judge decides. More often than not, though, the supervised parent will be ordered to pay for the cost. A.R.S. § 25-410.

6

Developing a Parenting Plan

In Arizona, parents can reach an agreement on a plan for legal decision-making authority and parenting time with their child, two main components in every required *parenting plan*. A.R.S. § 25-403.02. If parents cannot agree and custody is contested, then each must submit a proposed parenting plan to the court, effectively turning the issue over for the judge to decide.

The parenting plan is a blueprint for how the couple's child will be parented going forward. For many, arriving at a parenting plan is part of the custody proceedings in a divorce or legal separation. But parenting plans are of equal importance to unwed parents. A good parenting plan will guide both parents, helping everyone adjust in positive ways to life after the break-up.

The approved parenting plan is included in the judge's final orders. Should a parent violate the court's custody and parenting time orders, he or she may be held in contempt. The judge may order that missed parenting time be recovered, order parent education, and may assess court costs, civil penalties, and attorney fees against the violator. Additionally, the parties may be ordered back into mediation to resolve their conflicts, often at the violating parent's expense. A.R.S. § 25-414.

What Goes into the Parenting Plan?

All of the situations parents deal with day-to-day regarding their child should be addressed in the parenting plan. And every plan must be consistent with what is in that child's best interests (not what is in the parents' best interests).

According to A.R.S. § 25-403.02, at a minimum the couple's parenting plan should provide for the following:

1. *Designate whether both parents will have joint legal decision-making authority or whether one parent will have sole legal-decision making authority.*

2. What each parent's rights and responsibilities over the child's personal care will be; and over important decisions regarding education, healthcare, and religious upbringing.

3. A schedule for parenting time with the child, including holidays and school vacations.

4. A procedure for parenting time exchanges, including where exchanges will occur (location) and who will provide transportation.

5. A procedure mediating or resolving proposed changes, disputes, and alleged breaches, which may include private counseling, mediation, or use of court conciliation services.

6. A procedure for the parents' periodic review of their plan.

7. A procedure for parent communications regarding the child (how, when, how often).

8. A statement that each party has read, understands, and will abide by the notification requirements of A.R.S. § 25-403.05(B) regarding convicted or registered sex offenders or dangerous crimes against children.

9. Whenever a required element is absent from the parties' proposed parenting plan, the court will make adjustments. Furthermore, the judge has discretion to include additional provisions deemed necessary to promote and

protect the child.

To help you get started with your parenting plan, use this handy checklist:

- ✓ Who will be designated as having legal decision-making custody, or will you both have joint legal decision-making authority?

- ✓ Who will be responsible for your child's medical, dental, and optical care?

- ✓ What will be the parenting time schedule for weekdays, holidays, and vacations? (That's 24/7/365.)

- ✓ How will future problems or conflicts with the parenting plan be resolved?

- ✓ How will decisions be made about where your child will attend school?

- ✓ How will daycare be arranged?

- ✓ Who will take your child to school and pick your child up from school?

- ✓ Where and when will parenting time exchanges take place?

- ✓ How will your child's safety be ensured?

- ✓ How will both of you prevent your conflicts from harming your child?

- ✓ How will each of you maintain a nurturing, safe, and stable environment for your child?

✓ How will your child's basic needs (food, clothing, shelter), supervision, and emotional well-being be provided for?

✓ How will you help your child maintain a positive, healthy relationship with the other parent, and with other members of the family and community?

✓ How will your child's social, academic, athletic, or other activities be supported (within the parents' financial means)?

✓ How will extraordinary expenses be handled?

✓ What notification will be required in anticipation of a change to your child's residence?

As you can see, parenting plans cover every aspect of child-rearing. Although future modifications are sometimes necessary, a comprehensive plan that carefully addresses all contingencies can greatly diminish the need for court intervention later on. It's worth taking the time to try and get it right.

7

Strategies for Desired Custody

An experienced lawyer can offer strategies to help you get the custody arrangement you desire. There are no guarantees that the outcome will be precisely what you want, but there are several custody proceedings that can make a difference, beginning with temporary orders and the parenting conference.

First, either parent can file a motion asking the court to issue temporary orders providing for interim custody, parenting time, and support of a child, before any trial is even scheduled. Temporary orders can sometimes influence permanent orders later on. A.R.S. § 25-404.

When interim orders work well for a child, the court may be hesitant to upset the status quo when it comes time to enter permanent orders.

Second, a dispute resolution *parenting conference* may be scheduled in the high conflict case to help parents decide, for example, where their child will reside, how much time each parent will spend with the child, and how important decisions and day-to-day decisions will be made. The conciliator usually provides a written report to the judge with recommendations believed to be in the child's best interests.

Importantly, there are three alternative dispute resolution proceedings intended to help parents resolve their conflicts without the need for a trial. They include *mediation*, appointment of a *parenting coordinator*, and a *child custody evaluation*. Any or all of these proceedings may be part of your custody case.

How Do Mediators Help?

Arriving at a custody agreement with the other parent and avoiding trial is always possible with the help of a professional *mediator*. In Arizona, custody mediation is a confidential process, whether the mediator is assigned through the court's program or is a professional counselor in private practice. Mediated agreements are submitted to the judge who, absent objection, signs as an order. When mediation does not result in agreement to a parenting plan, the court will decide what is in the child's best interest and dictate custody terms to both parents.

How Do Parenting Coordinators Help?

In high conflict custody cases, a *parenting coordinator* may be appointed to meet with parents to discuss their concerns about the parenting plan. The coordinator does not advocate either party's position, but facilitates negotiations by blending counseling, parent-education, and dispute resolution techniques into the discussions.

As a facilitator, the coordinator assists parents in settling their differences to develop a parenting plan that is best for their child, while still satisfying as many of their individual needs as is reasonable and practical. If the parents cannot resolve their disputes and do not agree to a plan, then the coordinator will make recommendations to the court for custody orders. The judge may approve, modify, or reject those recommendations and may set the matter for hearing.

How Do Child Custody Evaluators Help?

After thorough investigation and inquiry in a limited scope psychological custody evaluation of the family, the *child custody evaluator* makes custody recommendations to the court. In determining what is in the child's best interests, the evaluator interviews the parents, the child, and other family members; and reviews documents and records regarding the child.

As a mental health professional, the evaluator submits a detailed report to the court with recommendations for legal decision-making and parenting time. When parents do not agree to a parenting plan and a custody trial becomes necessary, the evaluator's report will be very influential with the judge.

Tips for a Successful Relationship with Your Child

If custody is contested, your lawyer must present your parenting decisions and judgments in the light most favorable to you. The strategy is essential to your getting the relationship you want with your child. Even when parents are in agreement today, a custody disagreement could arise anytime. Therefore, always be prepared to validate and substantiate your parenting decisions –

before, during, and after your custody case is complete.

We have an excellent resource to help you obtain (and maintain) the parenting time you desire with your child. Our eBook, **PARENTING TO WIN: 7 Co-Parenting Tips for a Successful Relationship with Your Child,** is available upon request. In Parenting To Win, you will learn how to go about:

- Planning for what is in your child's best interests;

- Documenting your parenting time by keeping a parenting journal;

- Developing your plan for child care;

- Making the most of your parenting time;

- Making your home your child's home;

- Handling child support concerns without obstructing parenting time; and

- Taking precautions to protect your online privacy and reputation.

Acquire your copy of Parenting To Win by visiting www.ArizonaLawGroup.com for more information.

8

Orders for Child Support in Arizona

In every child custody case there will be a determination of child support. A.R.S. § 25-403.09. To determine how much support each parent must contribute, we go directly to the *Arizona Child Support Guidelines*. The calculations mandated by the guidelines base child support on specific criteria relating to the parents' income and the number of children residing in the home (but not the parents' living expenses).

When completing the child support worksheets, only the parents' income, parenting time, and expenses for the child's daycare, health insurance, and special needs are considered. Unless there are exceptional circumstances, ordinarily the court will follow the amount suggested by the guidelines.

As a parent, you need to know how support will be ordered for your child. To get an idea of the support obligation in your case and to begin budgeting, use the free child support calculator on our firm's website (www.ArizonaLawGroup.com) or download our free Arizona child support calculator apps for your iPhone and Android mobile devices.

Here is a checklist of the information you will need in order to use the child support calculator (if your figures aren't accurate, your results won't be either):

- ✓ Both parents' gross income;
- ✓ Spousal maintenance paid or received;
- ✓ Child's medical, dental, and vision insurance premiums;
- ✓ Court-ordered child support for children from other relationships;
- ✓ Expenses for child care and daycare;
- ✓ Extraordinary expenses for a child;
- ✓ Additional education expenses for a child;
- ✓ Parenting time travel expenses;

✓ Number of your children who are age 12 or older;

✓ Month and year of your youngest child's birthday;

✓ Number of parenting time days per year for each party; and

✓ Court-ordered arrears paid by the obligor-parent.

In any action involving child support, the amount calculated under the guidelines is presumed to be the amount the court shall order. However, the judge has discretion to make exceptions when results under the guidelines would be unjust or inappropriate given the circumstances. When exception is taken, the court may deviate from the guidelines by increasing or decreasing the amount of child support.

Lastly, the child support order includes the exact amount of support and the date payments shall begin. Be mindful that when a child emancipates, the obligor-parent should return to court and seek an order to modify or terminate support. A.R.S. § 25-320.

9

Modifying Child Custody Orders

The court's original custody orders may be modified under certain circumstances by evidencing a substantial and continuing change of circumstances. Either parent may request a change to legal decision-making authority, parenting time, or child support, or may seek to relocate with the child.

When May a Parent Ask for Custody Modification?

In general, the parent seeking modification must wait a full year from the date of the court's original order. But there are exceptional circumstances that allow a parent to request earlier modification, as follows:

- The parent can petition for modification if, after six months, the other parent has failed to comply with the joint legal decision-making order;

- The child is in an environment that could seriously endanger his or her physical, mental, moral or emotional health; or

- There is evidence that domestic violence, spousal abuse, or child abuse occurred after a joint legal decision-making order was entered.

For deployed service members, special rules may apply to modification of child custody. The court considers, for instance, the military parent's family care plan when determining what is best for the child during deployment. A.R.S. § 25-411.

What About Relocating with the Child?

When the judge ordered joint legal decision-making or parenting time and both parties reside in Arizona, the parent who desires to move more than 100 miles within Arizona or who desires to move out-of-state must provide written notice to the other parent 45 days in advance of the proposed child relocation. With few exceptions, the non-moving parent has 30 days after notice is made to file a petition with the court objecting to the child's relocation. A.R.S. § 25-408.

In determining whether relocation is in the child's best interests, the court considers all relevant factors, including:

- The circumstances that led to the parent's decision to move away;

- Whether the move could improve the quality of life enjoyed by the child and moving parent;

- The impact relocation will have on the other party's parenting time;

- Whether the move is motivated by a desire to keep the child away from the other parent;

- Whether the move is opposed in good faith;

- Whether the move is motivated by bad faith or a desire to gain an advantage with child support;

- Whether the moving parent is likely to comply with parenting time orders if relocation is granted; and

- How moving or not moving will affect the child's stability and emotional, physical, and developmental needs.

The parents can enter into a modified parenting time agreement, one that meets their primary objectives while still protecting each parent's relationship with the child. Longer but less frequent visits are a typical solution. Adjustments will need to be made to child support, with travel and lodging costs assigned, along with other expenses incurred, because of the non-moving parent's increased distance from the child. In the absence of an agreement, however, the court will decide the terms.

10

Domestic Violence, Child Abuse and Neglect

The court will not award joint legal decision-making authority if it finds significant domestic violence, or a history of such violence, by one parent against the other. Domestic violence is presumed to be contrary to the child's best interests.

If the court finds a parent committed an act of domestic violence, the parent must convince the judge that parenting time will not endanger the child or significantly impair the child's emotional development. If the parent meets this burden to the judge's satisfaction, then the court may require supervision and could place other conditions on parenting time to protect the child and the other parent from further harm. A.R.S. § 25-403.03.

Child abuse in Arizona is any conduct that causes physical, emotional, or psychological harm or injury to a minor, including sexual contact. Child neglect, which may or may not be coupled with abuse or domestic violence, deprives the minor of adequate food, clothing, shelter, or healthcare. Any history or incident of a parent's child abuse, child neglect, or domestic violence is a serious factor for the court to consider when determining legal decision-making authority and parenting time.

Stewart Law Group

11

Conclusion

In this book, we only touched on the essentials of child custody in Arizona. But nothing can replace specific legal advice from an experienced Arizona attorney. Now that you have reached the end, go back to Chapter 3 and take a more thoughtful look at what to consider when searching for a child custody lawyer to represent you.

The Stewart Law Group helps parents just like you successfully navigate child custody, often the most difficult legal and emotional challenge for a family to work through. With over six decades of combined experience, our legal team will provide the support and guidance you need so you can focus on what really matters – your children. Our family law attorneys represent mothers and fathers, divorcing parents, relocating parents, and unmarried parents on the full range of legal issues relating to child custody, legal decision-making, and parenting time in Arizona.

Stewart Law Group

Selected Arizona Statutes

§ 25-401. Definitions

In this chapter, unless the context otherwise requires:

1. "In loco parentis" means a person who has been treated as a parent by a child and who has formed a meaningful parental relationship with a child for a substantial period of time.

2. "Joint legal decision-making" means both parents share decision-making and neither parent's rights or responsibilities are superior except with respect to specified decisions as set forth by the court or the parents in the final judgment or order.

3. "Legal decision-making" means the legal right and responsibility to make all nonemergency legal decisions for a child including those regarding education, health care, religious training and personal care decisions. For the purposes of interpreting or applying any international treaty, federal law, a uniform code or the statutes of other jurisdictions of the U.S., legal decision-making means legal custody.

4. "Legal parent" means a biological or adoptive parent whose parental rights have not been terminated. Legal parent does not include a person whose paternity has not been established pursuant to § 25-812 or § 25-814.

5. "Parenting time" means the schedule of time during which each parent has access to a child at specified times. Each parent during their scheduled parenting time is responsible for providing the child with food, clothing and shelter and

may make routine decisions concerning the child's care.

6. "Sole legal decision-making" means one parent has the legal right and responsibility to make major decisions for a child.

7. "Visitation" means a schedule of time that occurs with a child by someone other than a legal parent.

§ 25-403. Legal Decision-Making and Best Interests of Child

A. The court shall determine legal decision-making and parenting time, either originally or on petition for modification, in accordance with the best interests of the child. The court shall consider all factors that are relevant to the child's physical and emotional well-being, including:

1. The past, present and potential future relationship between the parent and the child.

2. The interaction and interrelationship of the child with the child's parent or parents, the child's siblings and any other person who may significantly affect the child's best interest.

3. The child's adjustment to home, school and community.

4. If the child is of suitable age and maturity, the wishes of the child as to legal decision-making and parenting time.

5. The mental and physical health of all individuals involved.

6. Which parent is more likely to allow the child frequent, meaningful and continuing contact with the other parent. This paragraph does not apply if the court determines that a parent

is acting in good faith to protect the child from witnessing an act of domestic violence or being a victim of domestic violence or child abuse.

7. Whether one parent intentionally misled the court to cause an unnecessary delay, to increase the cost of litigation or to persuade the court to give a legal decision-making or a parenting time preference to that parent.

8. Whether there has been domestic violence or child abuse pursuant to § 25-403.03.

9. The nature and extent of coercion or duress used by a parent in obtaining an agreement regarding legal decision-making or parenting time.

10. Whether a parent has complied with Chapter 3, Article 5 of this Title.

11. Whether either parent was convicted of an act of false reporting of child abuse or neglect under § 13-2907.02.

B. In a contested legal decision-making or parenting time case, the court shall make specific findings on the record about all relevant factors and the reasons for which the decision is in the best interests of the child.

§ 25-403.02. Parenting Plans

A. If the child's parents cannot agree on a plan for legal decision-making or parenting time, each parent must submit a proposed parenting plan.

B. Consistent with the child's best interests in § 25-403 and §§ 25-403.03, 25-403.04 and 25-403.05, the court shall adopt a parenting plan that provides for both parents to share legal decision-making regarding their child and that maximizes their respective parenting time. The court shall not prefer a parent's proposed plan because of the parent's or child's gender.

C. Parenting plans shall include at least the following:

1. A designation of the legal decision-making as joint or sole as defined in § 25-401.

2. Each parent's rights and responsibilities for the personal care of the child and for decisions in areas such as education, health care and religious training.

3. A practical schedule of parenting time for the child, including holidays and school vacations.

4. A procedure for the exchanges of the child, including location and responsibility for transportation.

5. A procedure by which proposed changes, relocation of where a child resides with either parent pursuant to § 25-408, disputes and alleged breaches may be mediated or resolved, which may include the use of conciliation services or private counseling.

6. A procedure for periodic review of the plan's terms by the parents.

7. A procedure for communicating with each other about the child, including methods and frequency.

8. A statement that each party has read, understands and will abide by the notification requirements of § 25-403.05, subsection B.

D. If the parents are unable to agree on any element to be included in a parenting plan, the court shall determine that element. The court may determine other factors that are necessary to promote and protect the emotional and physical health of the child.

E. Shared legal decision-making does not necessarily mean equal parenting time.

§ 25-403.03. Domestic Violence and Child Abuse

A. Notwithstanding subsection D of this section, joint legal decision-making shall not be awarded if the court makes a finding of the existence of significant domestic violence pursuant to § 13-3601 or if the court finds by a preponderance of the evidence that there has been a significant history of domestic violence.

B. The court shall consider evidence of domestic violence as being contrary to the best interests of the child. The court shall consider the safety and well-being of the child and of the victim of the act of domestic violence to be of primary importance. The court shall consider a perpetrator's history of causing or threatening to cause physical harm to another person.

C. To determine if a person has committed an act of domestic violence the court, subject to the rules of evidence, shall consider all relevant factors including the following:

    1. Findings from another court of competent jurisdiction.

    2. Police reports.

    3. Medical reports.

    4. Records of the department of child safety.

5. Domestic violence shelter records.

6. School records.

7. Witness testimony.

D. If the court determines that a parent who is seeking sole or joint legal decision-making has committed an act of domestic violence against the other parent, there is a rebuttable presumption that an award of sole or joint legal decision-making to the parent who committed the act of domestic violence is contrary to the child's best interests. This presumption does not apply if both parents have committed an act of domestic violence. For the purposes of this subsection, a person commits an act of domestic violence if that person does any of the following:

1. Intentionally, knowingly or recklessly causes or attempts to cause sexual assault or serious physical injury.

2. Places a person in reasonable apprehension of imminent serious physical injury to any person.

3. Engages in a pattern of behavior for which a court may issue an ex parte order to protect the other parent who is seeking child custody or to protect the child and the child's siblings.

E. To determine if the parent has rebutted the presumption the court shall consider all of the following:

1. Whether the parent has demonstrated that being awarded sole or joint legal decision-making or substantially equal parenting time is in the child's best interests.

2. Whether the parent has successfully completed a batterer's prevention program.

3. Whether the parent has successfully completed a program of alcohol or drug abuse counseling, if the court determines that counseling is appropriate.

4. Whether the parent has successfully completed a parenting class, if the court determines that a parenting class is appropriate.

5. If the parent is on probation, parole or community supervision, whether the parent is restrained by a protective order that was granted after a hearing.

6. Whether the parent has committed any further acts of domestic violence.

F. If the court finds that a parent has committed an act of domestic violence, that parent has the burden of proving to the court's satisfaction that parenting time will not endanger the child or significantly impair the child's emotional development. If the parent meets this burden to the court's satisfaction, the court shall place conditions on parenting time that best protect the child and the other parent from further harm. The court may:

1. Order that an exchange of the child must occur in a protected setting as specified by the court.

2. Order that an agency specified by the court must supervise parenting time. If the court allows a family or household member to supervise parenting time, the court shall establish conditions that this person must follow during parenting time.

3. Order the parent who committed the act of domestic violence to attend and complete, to the court's satisfaction, a program of intervention for perpetrators of domestic violence

and any other counseling the court orders.

4. Order the parent who committed the act of domestic violence to abstain from possessing or consuming alcohol or controlled substances during parenting time and for twenty-four hours before parenting time.

5. Order the parent who committed the act of domestic violence to pay a fee for the costs of supervised parenting time.

6. Prohibit overnight parenting time.

7. Require a bond from the parent who committed the act of domestic violence for the child's safe return.

8. Order that the address of the child and the other parent remain confidential.

9. Impose any other condition that the court determines is necessary to protect the child, the other parent and any other family or household member.

G. The court shall not order joint counseling between a victim and the perpetrator of domestic violence. The court may provide a victim with written information about available community resources related to domestic violence.

H. The court may request or order the services of the department of child safety if the court believes that a child may be the victim of child abuse or neglect as defined in § 8-201.

I. In determining whether the absence or relocation of a parent shall be weighed against that parent in determining legal decision-making or parenting time, the court may consider whether the absence or relocation was caused by an act of domestic violence by the other parent.

§ 25-403.09. Child Support

A. For any parenting time order entered under this article, the court shall determine an amount of child support in accordance with § 25-320 and guidelines established pursuant to that section.

B. An award of joint legal decision-making or a substantially equal parenting time plan does not diminish the responsibility of either parent to provide for the support of the child.

§ 25-404. Temporary Orders

A. A party to a legal decision-making and parenting time proceeding may move for a temporary order. This motion must be supported by pleadings as provided in § 25-411. The court may award temporary legal decision-making and parenting time under the standards of § 25-403 after a hearing, or, if there is no objection, solely on the basis of the pleadings.

B. If a proceeding for dissolution of marriage or legal separation is dismissed, any temporary legal decision-making or parenting time order is vacated unless a parent or the child's custodian moves that the proceeding continue as a legal decision-making or parenting time proceeding and the court finds, after a hearing, that the circumstances of the parents and the best interest of the child require that a legal decision-making or parenting time plan decree be issued.

C. If a legal decision-making or parenting time proceeding commenced in the absence of a petition for dissolution of marriage or legal separation is dismissed, any temporary custody order thereby is vacated.

§ 25-803. Persons Who May Originate [Paternity] Proceedings; Legal Decision-Making; Parenting Time; Conciliation Court

A. Proceedings to establish the maternity or paternity of a child or children and to compel support under this article may be commenced by any of the following:

1. The mother.

2. The father.

3. The guardian, conservator or best friend of a child or children born out of wedlock.

4. A public welfare official or agency of the county where the child or children reside or may be found.

5. The state pursuant to § 25-509.

B. An adult may bring an action to establish the adult's biological parent.

C. Any party to a proceeding under this article other than the state may request that legal decision-making and specific parenting time be determined as a part of the proceeding. When paternity is established the court may award legal decision-making and parenting time as provided in § 25-408. The attorney general or county attorney shall not seek or defend any ancillary matters such as legal decision-making or parenting time.

D. In any case in which paternity is established the parent with whom the child has resided for the greater part of the last six months shall have legal decision-making unless otherwise ordered by the court.

E. The services of the conciliation court may be used in regard to disputed matters of legal decision-making and parenting time.

§ 25-1031. Initial Child Custody Jurisdiction

A. Except as otherwise provided in § 25-1034, a court of this state has jurisdiction to make an initial child custody determination only if any of the following is true:

1. This state is the home state of the child on the date of the commencement of the proceeding, or was the home state of the child within six months before the commencement of the proceeding and the child is absent from this state but a parent or person acting as a parent continues to live in this state.

2. A court of another state does not have jurisdiction under paragraph 1 or a court of the home state of the child has declined to exercise jurisdiction on the ground that this state is the more appropriate forum under § 25-1037 or 25-1038 and both of the following are true:

(a) The child and the child's parents, or the child and at least one parent or a person acting as a parent, have a significant connection with this state other than mere physical presence.

(b) Substantial evidence is available in this state concerning the child's care, protection, training and personal relationships.

3. All courts having jurisdiction under paragraph 1 or 2 have declined to exercise jurisdiction on the ground that a court of this state is the more appropriate forum to determine the custody of the child under § 25-1037 or 25-1038.

4. A court of any other state would not have jurisdiction under the criteria specified in paragraph 1, 2 or 3.

B. Subsection A of this section is the exclusive jurisdictional basis for making a child custody determination by a court of this state.

C. Physical presence of or personal jurisdiction over a party or a child is not necessary or sufficient to make a child custody determination.

About Scott David Stewart, Esq.

Born and raised in Phoenix, author Scott David Stewart, Esq., is the founder of the Stewart Law Group. With a select legal team, Mr. Stewart's vision was to establish a unique law firm singularly focused on the clients' experiences when dealing with difficult and often intensely emotional legal matters. Stewart Law Group represents clients in all matters of divorce, child custody, and family law.

Early in his career, Mr. Stewart was a Deputy County Attorney in the Major Crimes Division of the Maricopa County Attorney's Office. While there, Mr. Stewart honed his trial skills and developed the strategies for success that he continuously implements in all aspects of his law practice today. Since its formation, Stewart Law Group has earned the trust and respect of clients from all walks of life.

Mr. Stewart is a member of the State Bar of Arizona, Maricopa County Bar Association, and American Bar Association. He has an AV Preeminent® attorney-rating from Martindale-Hubbell® and is also rated "Superb" by Avvo, Inc. With more than 65 years of combined legal experience, Mr. Stewart and the attorneys with the Stewart Law Group are prepared to take on the most complex and challenging cases.

About Amy E. Dohrendorf, Esq.

As an Arizona divorce and family lawyer, Amy E. Dohrendorf, Esq., is truly in her element. She enjoys helping all of her clients through their legal challenges, no matter how difficult. Her obvious passion for the work she does and high level of preparedness, courtroom skill, and diligence are recognized by clients and peers alike.

"I was born to be a lawyer." That was the beautifully framed quotation Ms. Dohrendorf's father gave her at graduation. She has always wanted to be an attorney. As a child, she engaged her parents in spirited debates over everything from current events, to curfew restrictions, to what she should eat for dinner.

What motivated her to practice divorce and family law? Her parents divorced when she was a child, but they did so amicably and civilly, respectful of each other as individuals. As a result, both she and her brother grew up as well-adjusted children of divorce. Compassionate, professional, and thorough, today she assists her clients in achieving the best possible outcome under Arizona law, for themselves and for their children.

Ms. Dohrendorf graduated from NAU with a Bachelor's Degree in Communications, cum laude. She received her Juris Doctorate from the University of Denver, Sturm College of Law. Early in her legal career, she was a Deputy Public Defender in the Maricopa County Public Defender's Office. Thereafter, Ms. Dohrendorf was in private family law practice for years before joining the legal team at Stewart Law Group where she is now partner. Her office is located at the law firm's Chandler, Arizona, location.

Stewart Law Group

777 E Thomas Rd Ste 210, Phoenix AZ 85014
Phone: 602.548.4600

1490 S Price Rd Ste 212, Chandler AZ 85286
17470 N Pacesetter Way, Scottsdale AZ 85255
14050 N 83rd Ave Ste 290, Peoria AZ 85381
1910 S Stapley Dr Ste 221, Mesa AZ 85204
20325 N 51st Ave Ste 134, Glendale AZ 85308

www.ArizonaLawGroup.com

Made in USA - Crawfordsville, IN
25759_9780988605237
04.09.2020 0535